GOOOAAALLL!

By Chris McTrustry

Illustrated by Rob Kiely

GOOOAAALL

Predict: What do you think this text is going to be about?

I WAS DETERMINED this year would be different.

This year I would be selected for the school soccer team. No more "no thanks, try again next year, Gabriel". This would be my year. After all, great soccer playing was in my blood. I was named after my Uncle Gabriel, who was a star soccer player. He even played for a European soccer team. Sadly, he died in a car accident.

So, I'm determined to carry on the family tradition of soccer stardom!

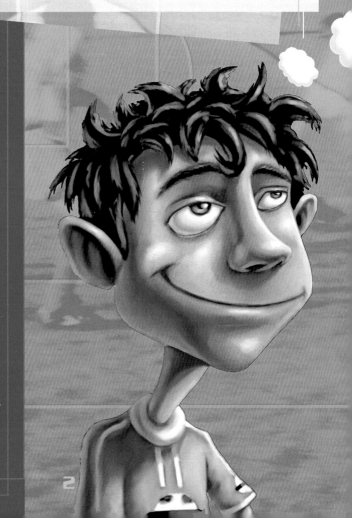

2

Unfortunately, my feet don't agree with me. Don't get me wrong, I practise. I like playing. I just don't ... 'get' soccer.

"It'll come to you," my Tata (grandpa) said. He used to be a good player too, and he's always ready with advice and tips. I'd 'hired' him – paying him with odd jobs around his and Abuelita's (grandma's) house – to prepare me for the upcoming trials.

A week before the trials I was nosing around in Tata's garden shed. At the back of the shed I found a pair of old, cracked soccer boots, abandoned like empty cicada cases.

"Those were your Uncle Gabriel's when he was about your age," Tata said when I showed them to him. "Try them on." He grinned. "Maybe a little of his magic will rub off on you."

...ABANDONED LIKE EMPTY CICADA CASES...

Simile or Metaphor?

Simile – creates a mind picture in which one thing is said to be like another. The words *like* or *a* are used to make the comparison

Metaphor – creates a mind picture in which one thing is described as if it were actually that thing.

So… I put the boots on. And do you know what? When I had Uncle Gabriel's boots on my feet I did feel quite different. Confident. Balanced. Focused.

I tried some of the dribbling tricks Tata had shown me.

"Hey! What do you know?!" Tata whooped. "I think you've got it! Kewell or even Viduka couldn't have done that move better!"

I didn't say anything but I knew that a little of Uncle G's 'magic' must have seeped into the cracked leather of the boots.

Gabriel trying on Uncle G's boots

? Question?

Why do you think Gabriel felt different?

ACTION AND RESPONSE CHART

Gabriel trying some tricks

Action

Gabriel put his boots on

Response

Confident, balanced and focused

Find another action and response

For the rest of the week I practised like nobody's business. Tata watched from the sidelines like a hawk surveying its prey.

"Stick to the basic stuff," Tata advised me.

I watched soccer videos (wearing Uncle G's magical boots), and concentrated hard on positional play.

"A lot of young guys just chase the ball," Tata said. "If you stay in position or anticipate where the ball's going to go, you can get a lot of kicks. Think before you run. Think before you kick."

I nodded my head. "Good idea, Tata."

Question?

I practised like nobody's business.

What does this mean?

Gabriel practising his move

"THINK BEFORE YOU KICK."

SURVEYING

Which is the synonym?

A observing carefully

B glancing

C looking

A, B or C ?

Gabriel and Tata

Video time!

Question?

Why do you think Gabriel watched the videos with his boots on?

Monday morning was the day. Soccer trials.

"What are you doing here, Gabriel?" Marco Cavallaro smirked sarcastically. "Trying out for Team Orange Peeler?"

Before I could think of a comeback, Mr Timpano, the team coach, called us together. "Okay, lads," he said. "Some of you won't make the team, but don't be disappointed. Do your best and play fair."

Okay. I'll cut straight to the BIG news. I got picked. Yes! I was in the school soccer team. And it was all thanks to Uncle G's 'magical' boots.

Mr Timpano couldn't believe my improvement. He called me 'a hardworking mid-fielder, with loads of flair and potential'.

Trying out for
Team orange Peeler
What does this mean?

During the games, I stuck to my position like a limpet sticks to a rock. I let Uncle G's boots guide me. I set up a lot of goals for our team. But what I really wanted was to score my own goal. How cool would that be?!

Unbelievably, we fought our way into the final of the Inter-Schools Competition! The whole school was coming to watch us play Cairncross, a school with an excellent soccer team.

CHARACTER PROFILE

What words best describe Gabriel?

ambitious	pessimistic
determined	nervous
calm	selfish
courteous	positive
excitable	optimistic

WE FOUGHT OUR WAY

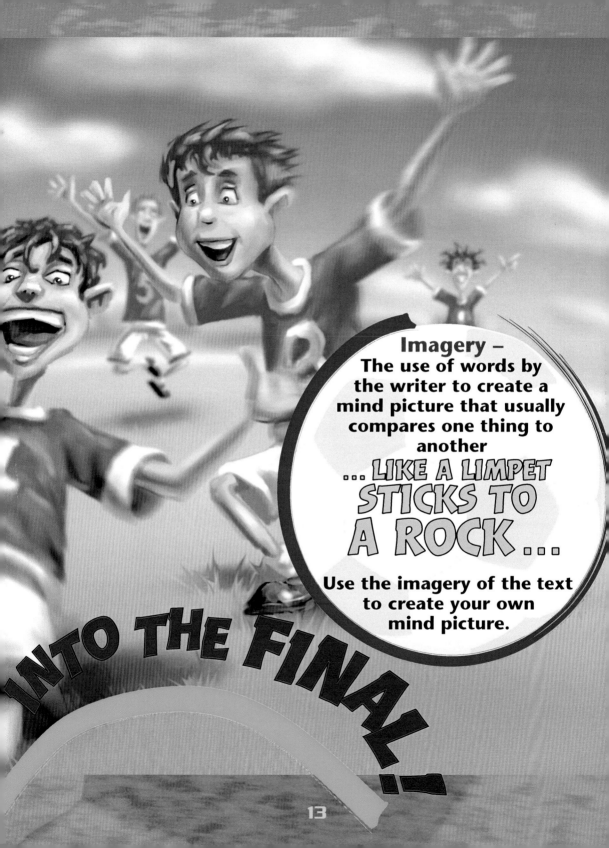

Imagery –
The use of words by
the writer to create a
mind picture that usually
compares one thing to
another

**... LIKE A LIMPET
STICKS TO
A ROCK ...**

Use the imagery of the text
to create your own
mind picture.

INTO THE FINAL!

I COULDN'T HELP

The day of the final finally arrived.

I got up early. I was too excited to sleep. I played on the computer. Then I read a book. But all the while I was willing time to move on QUICKLY. The sooner I was at the ground – on the field – the better.

"Okay, Gabriel," Mum said at last. "Get your boots. It's time to go."

Yes! But my boots weren't in their usual spot. I couldn't help it – I screamed. LOUD.

Mum and Dad rushed to me.

Question?

What can be inferred about Gabriel's character from the words:

'MY BOOTS WEREN'T IN THEIR USUAL SPOT'

IT – I SCREAMED.

"What's the matter?" Mum shrilled.

"Where are they?" I said frantically. "I can't find them – my boots!"

Mum smiled. "That's because Dad and I have a surprise for you."

I frowned. "I don't know if Cup Final Day is the day for surprises, Mum … please, can I just have my boots?"

Dad appeared in the doorway holding a brightly wrapped box. "Surprise, mate!"

"This is our way of saying well done," Mum said.

FRANTICALLY

Which is the synonym?

A excitedly

B desperately

C calmly

A, B or C ?

Under the wrapping paper was a shoebox. A cold feeling swept over me like a blast of Arctic wind. Oh no … inside the box was a brand new pair of SOCCER BOOTS.

"Thanks, ummm … but, where are *my* boots?" I demanded.

"You can't wear those tatty old things in the final," Mum said. "Everyone will laugh!"

Mum didn't know how right she was. Everyone *would* laugh – at me! I'd play hopelessly without Uncle G's magic boots.

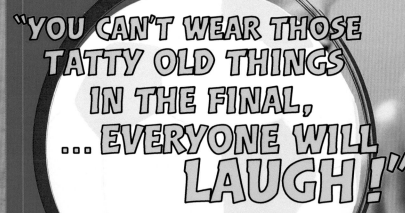

"YOU CAN'T WEAR THOSE TATTY OLD THINGS IN THE FINAL, ... EVERYONE WILL LAUGH!"

What inference can be drawn about Mum from this text?

Well, I wasn't letting anyone down. On the field I avoided the ball as if it were contaminated. If I didn't kick it, I couldn't do any harm, right?

I must have been obvious, because at half time Mr Timpano said, "Gabriel, if you're trying to lull the Cairncross team into a false sense of security, you've done it. Now start playing – properly." I nodded. "Yes, Coach."

But I continued to avoid the ball. I drifted out onto the left wing and 'hid'. Occasionally the ball would be booted my way. Each time I simply trapped it and punched passes through the centre of the Cairncross defence. One of my passes found our centre forward, Tran Nguyen. He beat the centre half and shot. The Cairncross goalkeeper dived full length and tipped the ball out of play. That was the closest anyone on either team came to scoring.

?Question?
...false sense of security...
What is meant by this?

Late in the game, Wayne Butler ran down the right wing. He beat two defenders and shaped to cross the ball. All of our forwards and midfielders raced into the penalty area, anticipating Wayne's cross. I was going to join them when, suddenly, I realised that if the ball was crossed high Cairncross's centre half would easily clear the ball. With most of our team in the Cairncross penalty area, we'd be an easy target for a fast breakaway. I hesitated on the edge.

"What are you doing, Gabriel?" Mr Timpano yelled. "There's less than a minute left! Get into the penalty area!"

SETTING

What words would you use to describe the atmosphere at the game?

Tense	Quiet
Dull	Noisey
Calm	Serene
Lively	**What Else?**

"... LESS THAN

A MINUTE LEFT !"

But something – a message from Uncle G's boots? – told me to stay where I was. And the words of my Tata reverberated in my head – "Think before you run. Think before you kick."

Wayne whipped in a high cross. Marco Cavallaro jumped up to head it but he was easily beaten by the Cairncross centre half.

The ball bounced out to me. I measured my stride and smashed the ball back into the penalty area. The ball left my foot like it was jet-propelled, and flew into the top right-hand corner of Cairncross's goal.

I, me, Gabriel Gomez, had scored, all by myself, with *my* boots. Before I knew it, the referee blew for full time. We had won!

WE HAD WON!

Clarify!

REVERBERATED

A repeated

B appeared

C bounced

A, B or C ?

Question?

The ball left my foot
like it was jet-propelled...

What does this mean?

Mum and Dad, Tata and Abuelita hurried up to congratulate me.

"Well done, my boy," Tata grinned. He nodded at my new boots. "I see you've upgraded your footwear."

"I wanted to wear Uncle G's boots," I shrugged, "but Mum and Dad got me these for playing so well."

"Good thing, too," Tata said. "You know those 'magic' boots you found?" I nodded. "They weren't your Uncle Gabriel's after all." He pointed at Dad. "They were your Dad's." He laughed. "And he was downright hopeless!"

Select the main points you would include in a summary of Goal.

'MAGIC' BOOTS

THINK ABOUT THE TEXT

Making connections – What connections can you make
to the emotions, situations or characters in *Goal!*?

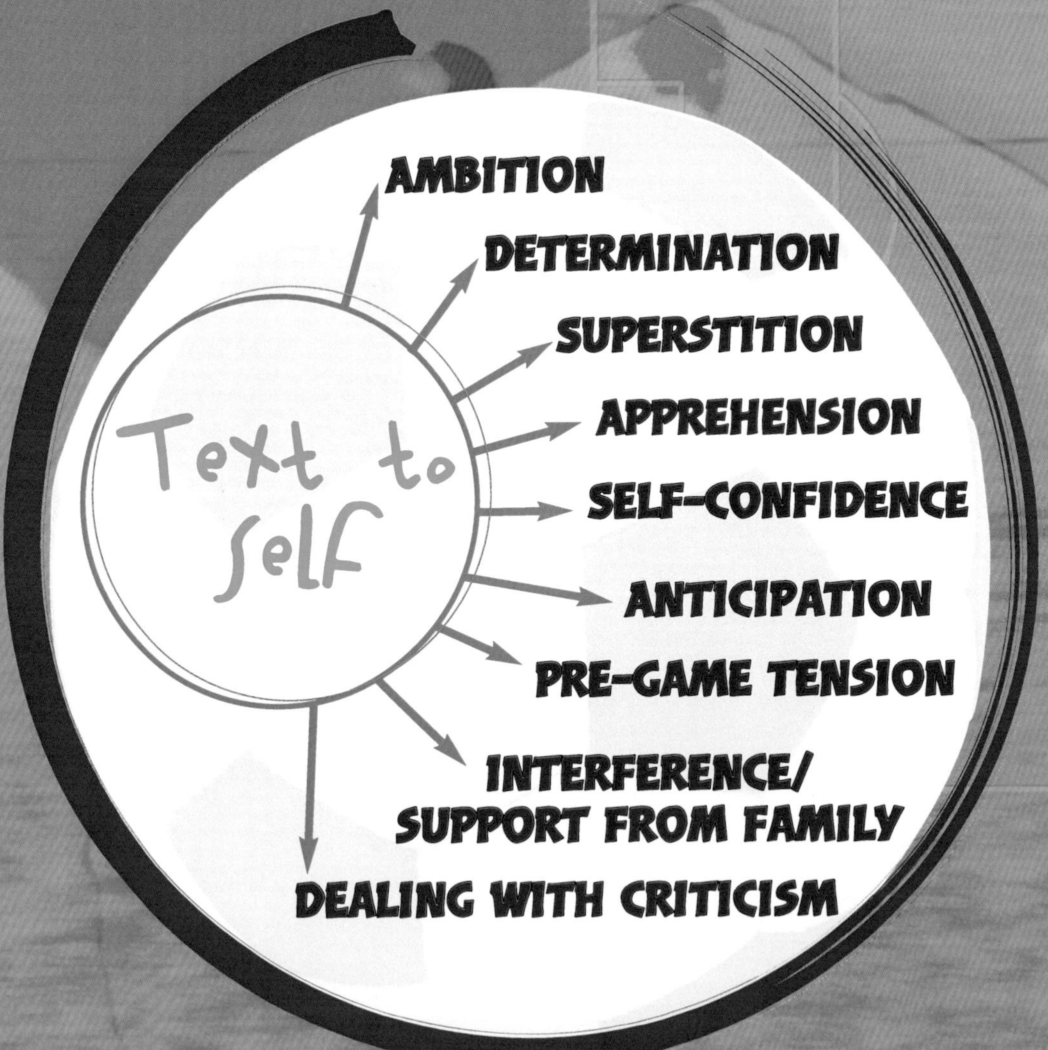

Text to
Self

AMBITION

DETERMINATION

SUPERSTITION

APPREHENSION

SELF-CONFIDENCE

ANTICIPATION

PRE-GAME TENSION

INTERFERENCE/
SUPPORT FROM FAMILY

DEALING WITH CRITICISM

Text to Text

Talk about other stories you may have read that have similar features. Compare the stories.

Text to World

Talk about situations in the world that might connect to elements in the story.

PLANNING A SHORT STORY

1 Decide on a Storyline

A boy finds an old pair of soccer boots that he believes belonged to his uncle, a great soccer player.

↓

He thinks that the boots have 'magic' that will make him a great soccer player too.

↓

He discovers that the boots actually belonged to someone who didn't play soccer very well.

2 Think about the Characters

Think about the way they will think, act and feel.
Make some short notes or quick sketches.

GABRIEL

**enthusiastic
determined
persistent**

GRANDFATHER

**supportive
interested
helpful**

MUM

**concerned
proud
caring**

3 Decide on the setting

Make some short notes.

4 Decide on the Events in order

Introduction

Events

Climax

SHORT STORIES USUALLY HAVE

A A short introduction that grabs the reader's interest.

B Fewer characters than longer stories.

C A single fast-moving plot.

D A climax that occurs late in the story.